1

2

The Big RSPB

David Chandler

Birdwatch

Get to know the birds outside **your** window!

A&C Black • London

This book is for Nina, Matthias and Thomas Crofton. Please show it to your teachers. Then ask them if you can do the Big Schools' Birdwatch!

Published 2011 by
A&C Black,
Bloomsbury Publishing PLC
49-51 Bedford Square,
London
WC1B 3DP

ISBN 978-1-4081-4821-1

A CIP catalogue for this book is available from the British Library.

Design and illustration: Geoff Ward

Printed in China by Toppan Leefung.

Picture credits: All photographs by Shutterstock except: p16–17, p60, RSPB; p54, David Chandler; p73, p81, p88, p93, p117, iStockphoto; p86–87, p95, p102, p111, p120, Corbis Images; p87, Getty Images; p101, p104–105, p115, p116–117, Super Stock.

Hello!

Welcome to this book. You might be wondering what it's all about. Have you heard of the Big Schools' Birdwatch, or the Big Garden Birdwatch? You may even have done one of them. This book will help you take part. It will also help you to enjoy watching birds all year round, with amazing nature activities and fascinating bird facts.

A big chunk of it looks at 25 different types of bird that you're most likely to see on your birdwatch. These pages will help you work out which type of bird you are looking at. But they do more than that. They tell you something about the birds too. There are some awesome facts in here. That's because birds do some amazing things.

We've also crammed in lots of things for you to do. You could make your own field guide, build your own nest, plant a tree, invent a game, act like a bird or become a species expert.

What else? Want to know how to be a bird watcher? We'll help you. Not sure what feathers are for? The answers are here. Would you like to know how birds find their way to Africa? Turn to page 58. You don't have to start at the beginning and finish at the end. It's not that kind of book.

One more thing. I know this is meant to be a book for children. But I think quite a lot of adults will like it too. Show it to your teacher. Show it to the grown-ups at home. But make sure they don't keep it for too long. It's your book! Now get reading.

David Chandler

Contents

Be part of something huge – a Big Birdwatch!

Why would you want to go birdwatching with lots of other people? It would be noisy and you wouldn't see many birds. This big birdwatch is different. Hundreds of thousands of people do it and they see millions of birds. You can be one of those people.

It's easy to do, doesn't take very long, and what you see helps scientists know what's happening to our birds. There are two ways you can do it.

The Big Schools' Birdwatch

This is a birdwatch especially for schools and youth groups. In 2011, nearly 90,000 children and teachers took part!

Talk to one of your teachers and ask them if you can do it. If your school wants to take part, they need to tell the RSPB. They can do this on the RSPB website from the end of September. Then they will be sent a pack containing everything your school or group needs to take part. There are also lots of fun activities on the website for your group to do together.

You can do the birdwatch on any day in the second half of January. All you have to do is watch the birds in your school grounds or a park for one hour. Well, you do have to do a bit of counting too, but that's part of the fun. You have to work out what types of birds you see, and count them. For each type, you count the most you can see at once. Then you tell the RSPB what you saw. Don't forget to send back your results.

You and your teacher can find out more on the RSPB website: **www.rspb.org.uk/schoolswatch/**

The Big Garden Birdwatch

The Big Garden Birdwatch takes place on the last weekend of January. You can do it with your family or friends, in any garden or park. Watch the birds for one hour, and write down the highest number of each type of bird you see. Then let the RSPB know what you saw.

You and your family can find out more on the RSPB website: **www.rspb.org.uk/birdwatch/**

If you're really keen, you could do both!

Name that bird

You're looking at a bird. You don't know what it is. How do you work out what you're looking at?

You need to be a smart detective, and collect the clues that will tell you the answer. And it's as easy as RSPB…

R

'R' stands for **record**. Make a note of what you notice so you don't forget. A quick sketch (see page 24) is a good way to do this. Remember to write down where and when you saw it too.

S

The 'S' is for **shape and size**. What shape is the bird? I don't mean round or square. Is it duck-shaped? Sparrow-shaped? Pigeon-shaped? How long are its legs? What shape is its beak?

And how big is the bird? Blackbird-sized? As big as a swan? Or you could say it's as big as a fizzy drink can or a football. You get the idea.

P

Now you know what shape it is and roughly how big it is. 'P' stands for **pattern**. What colours and markings can you see on the bird? And where? Write it down or add it to your sketch.

B

The 'B' is for **behaviour**. Not yours, the bird's. What is it doing? Is it hovering over the grass by the road like a kestrel? Tossing leaves over with its beak like a blackbird? Smashing a snail like a song thrush? What a bird does can help you know what it is. Watch how it moves and flies. Does it walk, run or hop? Fly in a straight line or bounce up and down?

Don't give up if you can't work out every bird you see. The more you practise the better you will get.

There are other clues that can help you. Listen to any noises it makes. Some bird watchers can name birds just by hearing them. If you practise, you will be able to do that too.

Where and when you saw the bird is important too. Lots of bird books have maps that show you where birds live. If you think you know what you saw, make sure it lives where you saw it.

The habitat is a clue. You won't see a woodpecker swimming on a lake or a swan climbing up a tree trunk. And not all birds are here all the time. Some of them have a winter home. There won't be any swifts here in December.

When you've got all your clues, use a book or website to help you name your bird. If you see a bird at school or in your garden, start with the birds in this book. If it's not there, you could try looking on the RSPB's website.

You can also use the Spotter's Guide at the back of this book to help you!

Plant a tree

This is something you can do to help wildlife that could last for a very long time. Some trees live for hundreds of years. That's even older than your head teacher!

Why?

Trees do lots of good things. Birds nest in them, find food on them and sleep in them. Minibeasts live in them and eat bits of them. Trees help you breathe more easily. They give off oxygen and we all need that. They make the world look better too.

TREE TIPS

These trees are good for wildlife. The funny words in italics are their scientific names. You could use this list to help you to buy the right type of tree.

Little ones
Elder   *Sambucus nigra*
Rowan   *Sorbus aucuparia*
Bird Cherry   *Prunus padus*

Bigger ones, but not whoppers
Field Maple   *Acer campestre*
Wild Cherry   *Prunus avium*
Alder   *Alnus glutinosa*
Silver Birch   *Betula pendula*

Whoppers (plant these at least 15 metres away from buildings)
Common Oak   *Quercus robur*
Sessile Oak   *Quercus petraea*
Hornbeam   *Carpinus betulus*
Beech   *Fagus sylvatica*

So what do I plant?

A tree or a shrub (another word for a bush). Find out which ones grow in the wild near where you want to plant it. It's a good idea to plant one of those.

Plant your tree between October and March. This is when the trees are 'sleeping', so they don't mind being moved. At that time of the year you can plant trees with bare roots.

Here's what you do

- Dig a hole. Make sure it's big enough to hold all the roots.
- Put the tree in the middle of the hole.
- Cover the roots with soil. Push the soil down firmly.
- Make sure the soil is level at the top. If it dips down, water will collect there and that won't help your tree. Add some soil from somewhere else if you need to top it up a bit.

Try to stop other plants growing too near your tree. Pull up any that grow closer than about 50cm. Or cover the ground with something to stop them growing. This makes it easier for your tree to get food and water from the soil, because the other plants aren't sucking it up too. Ask a grown-up to help you. You don't need to water your tree in the winter. But you could water it in its first spring and summer.

What do you call a robin that can sew?

A bobbin

Build your own nest

Birds build some really cool nests. Long-tailed tits build a wonderful ball of moss, spiders' webs, feathers and lichen. Ospreys build huge stick nests and a great crested grebe's nest can float! But not all birds are ace nest-builders. Collared doves need some nest-building lessons! All they do is make a flimsy nest of twigs. There are lots of gaps in it and sometimes the eggs fall through the holes. Maybe you could do better…

Go outside and find some natural materials – twigs, grass, leaves, and whatever else you think you need to make a safe, cosy nest. Please don't pull plants up to make your nest, or pull bits off anything alive! Then make your nest. It's easiest to make it on the ground.

Did you hear about the duck decorator?
He papered over the quacks

Hide yourself!

Wouldn't it be great to be invisible? You could get up to all sorts of tricks. Imagine how close you could get to birds. Sorry, we can't make you invisible. But we can help you to hide.

How to disappear

Wear clothes that are dull, natural colours – greens, browns and blacks are good. Don't wear your bright orange cycling gear! That would scare everything off!

Then find a place where you can wait for birds to come to you. Somewhere they feed would be good, or somewhere in a wood, or by the side of a pond. Don't forget to let a grown-up know where you are going. Or you could find some birds, then creep up on them, maybe crawling on your belly. But please don't do any of this near a bird's nest.

To really disappear, cover your hands and face too. Dark gloves will hide your hands. You could put a blanket over your head, but then you wouldn't see anything. A hat with a scarf wrapped around your face is better.

Wear clothes that will help you to blend in.

Advanced hiding

Use some face-paints. Put them on like camouflage. But don't do this if you're allergic to face-paints – that would be silly! Go for greens, browns, black, and other dull colours.

Make a camo-net

Disappear outdoors! A camo-net will make you harder to see against the trees and bushes. Here's how to make one.

You'll need some old garden netting. Remember to ask a grown-up first before you borrow it. Stick leaves and twigs in it, or tie them on. Or tie on strips of natural coloured material. Then hide under your new camo-net. Why not sit on a fold-up stool, with the net over you? That way you won't get as cold and wet.

Test your camouflage by hiding somewhere and seeing if your friends can find you. Make sure a grown-up knows what you're up to and don't stay hidden forever!

How does a bird with a broken wing manage to land?
By sparrow-chute

A camo-net will help you to disappear.

Build a hide

Lots of proper nature reserves have 'hides'.
These are like sheds with narrow windows.
You lift a flap and look out through the slit.
The birds can't see you but you can see them.
Here are some ways to make your own.

Through a window

Find a window that looks out on a place where
a lot of birds gather – maybe near a bird table or
feeder. Get a big bit of cardboard or thick paper.
Cut some flaps in it that you
can fold up, for taking a peep
at the birds. Now stick it on
the inside of the window,
so it covers most of the
glass. Make sure you have
permission to do this.

> What do you call
> a bird being silly?
> **A great twit**

In a box

Use a very big cardboard
box. It should be big enough
for you and your best mate
to squeeze into. Cut flaps
in it so you can look out
of it. To make it harder to
see, you could paint it or
stick leaves or twigs on it. It
won't last forever, but when
it goes soggy you can get
another box.

How about using a shed as
a hide instead?

Birds through binoculars

It's easy. Find some birds and watch them.
Now you're a bird watcher! But when you get
hooked, you'll want to see the birds better.
To do that you will need binoculars.

Eyepiece

Binoculars

Binoculars make things look closer
than they are. Choose a pair that
make things look six to eight times
closer. You can find this out by
looking at the numbers on the
binoculars. An 8x32 makes things
look eight times closer.

Look through the binoculars and
make sure the view is nice and
clear. Make sure they aren't too big
and heavy for you. Most binoculars
are made for grown-ups. This means
that the eyepieces might not come
close enough together for your
eyes. Make sure they do or they
won't work properly for you.

If you have to wear glasses
when you are using
binoculars, twist or
fold the eyecups
down and test this
out too. Not all
binoculars work
well with glasses.

Focussing wheel

Eyecup

Eyepiece
adjuster

Setting them up

Have a look at your binoculars. There's a big main wheel in the middle for making the picture sharp. Have a look at the right eyepiece. There will be a way of adjusting it so that the binoculars work well for your eyes. This is because your left eye might be different to your right eye. The adjuster might be a wheel under the eyepiece. Or the eyepiece might turn. If you can't see it, check the instructions to find out where it is.

Here's what you do to get the best picture:

- Cover up the right side so that you can only see down the left side.
- Look at something sharp 50–100 metres away, like a TV aerial or chimney.
- Turn the big wheel in the middle until the view is nice and clear.
- Now cover the left side and look down the right side only.
- Adjust the right eyepiece until the picture is nice and clear. Don't do this with the wheel in the middle – use the eyepiece adjuster.
- That's it. Leave the binoculars set like that.
- Now it should be clear on both sides just by turning the big wheel in the middle.

Where's the bird gone?

At first you can see the bird. You pick up your binoculars and look through them. But then you can't find the bird again. It takes practice to get good with binoculars. When you see a bird, keep looking at it. Lift your binoculars to your eyes without taking your eyes off the bird. Sometimes, of course, the bird really has flown away!

Carry the binoculars on their strap around your neck. It makes it easy to grab them quickly when you see an exciting bird.

Objective lens

Sound advice

Here's a top tip to make you a better bird watcher. Learn some bird noises. This way you will know which bird is singing that song, or calling that call. It's not easy to learn sounds from books. So how do you do it?

Take a nature walk

This is a great way to learn, but it takes time. When you hear a bird singing, look for it until you find it. Work out what it is. Then match what you hear with what you see.

Make a memory hook

Use your own words to describe a bird noise. For example, 'chack chack chack'. You could use the descriptions in the Spotter's Guide on pages 74–125 to help you. Or say things like 'made a noise like stones being knocked together', or 'sounded like water tumbling down a rocky stream'.

You could give it a silly sentence to help you remember the song. A yellowhammer is meant to sound like it's saying 'a little bit of bread and no cheese'.

It doesn't matter how you do it – if it helps you remember the noise it's okay!

WHY DO BIRDS SING?

In the bird world, the boys do most of the singing. There are two things they are trying to say. 'I'm cool and handsome and I'd be a great bird to have some eggs with'. That's for the girls. They are not as friendly to the other boys. They hear 'Oi you, this is my patch. Get out of here!'

Use some gizmos

Listen to recorded bird noises to help you learn the calls and to check what you heard. The RSPB website has lots of bird noises on it. There are also CDs, DVDs and apps you can buy.

Map it

Draw a 'x' in the middle of a bit of paper or card. Sit quietly for a few minutes and note down the noises around you. Try to work out what some of the birds are. Do it again in the same place two or three weeks later. You might find the same birds singing from the same place. That's because it's one of their song-posts – a place they sing from again and again.

Elephant ears

To help you hear birds better, cup your hands behind your ears. Point your head at a singing bird. Its song will sound louder and clearer. You can use this trick to help you work out where a noise is coming from. Turn your head from side to side – when the sound is loudest you are looking the right way.

What is an owl's phone number?
282820

WHEN TO LEARN

Lots of birds sing in spring. That makes it a tricky time to start to learn. There's so much bird noise that it's hard to sort them out. It's easier to start earlier in the year. Some birds sing then – for example, robins, wrens, dunnocks and song thrushes. There are fewer noises to confuse you. Also, a lot of trees won't have leaves yet so it's easier to see the birds.

If you map the birds you see, you might find them again.

Lift off!

Most birds fly and they are very good at it. To stay in the air they need 'lift'. This is a force that pushes them up. Birds get lift by flapping their wings and by the holding their wings with the back edge lower than the front. The shape of a bird's wing is very important too.

It's a special shape. If you cut through it and looked at it from the end, it would look like this.

This shape is called an aerofoil. Aeroplane wings are the same sort of shape. But birds got their wings sorted out a long time before aeroplanes did! When this shape moves forward through the air, it gets lifted up. You can see this for yourself.

6 Poke it through the top surface a bit nearer the front. When you hold the cotton up straight, the back end of the wing should hang down.

7 Here's the fun bit. Get someone to hold the cotton up straight. Take a deep breath. Blow hard on the front of the wing. The wing will go up the cotton. It won't go all the way up unless you have lungs as big as a whale. But it will go up a bit. Don't blow too hard or you'll feel wobbly.

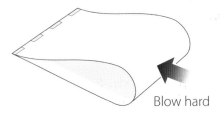

Blow hard

1 Get an A4 piece of paper.

2 Fold it like this. Don't put a crease in the front edge. Keep it curved.

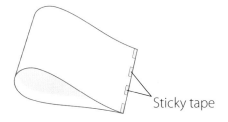

Sticky tape

3 Use small bits of sticky tape to hold the paper in this shape. If you've done it right it should look like an aerofoil shape.

4 Ask a grown-up for a needle and some cotton.

5 Poke the needle through the bottom surface of your 'wing', roughly in the middle.

Here's another way of showing the same thing. You need a book and a bit of paper. Stick the paper in the book so that lots of it hangs down at the back. That's a bit like a wing shape too. Hold the book near your mouth and blow under the book. Of course the paper goes up. Now blow over the top. Hah! It went up then too.

When a bird's wings move through the air, they go up – just like your bits of paper. That's why birds don't fall out of the sky.

In the summertime

There are some birds that you can hear or see in the summer that aren't around when you do the Big Schools' Birdwatch or the Big Garden Birdwatch in the winter. Most of them are small birds that spend the winter in Africa.

Swift

Swifts look like dark flying anchors. Look up to see them. You might hear their screeching calls as they race each other across the skies. Swifts are champion flyers. They get here in April and May, and they are gone again in August.

Swallow

Learn how to tell swallows from swifts and martins and you'll look like a real bird watcher. It's not too hard. Swallows are mostly pale underneath and blue-black on top. Look for their lovely long tail streamers. Their winter home is in South Africa, 6000 miles away. Imagine flying there and back every year!

Swallows have long tail streamers. House martins don't.

House martin

A house martin's back is a blue-black colour. They are white underneath. Look for a bright white bit at the bottom of their backs. House martins have forked tails but without long streamers like a swallow has. They live in mud nests at the top of the wall under the edge of the roof. If there's not enough mud, it's hard for them to build a nest.

The best way to tell a willow warbler from a chiffchaff is its song.

Willow warbler and chiffchaff

These two birds look a lot like each other. They both live in trees and bushes. Look for a chiffchaff's black legs to tell them apart. They aren't always easy to see and you'll need a very good view to see their legs. But they are easy to hear! Have a listen to their songs on the RSPB website. That's the easiest way to tell them apart.

Cuckoo

This is a bird with a famous song. You might hear one, but it's very hard to see one. Cuckoos are famous for laying eggs in the nests of other birds, and letting these birds bring up the young cuckoos.

How to draw a bird

Birds come from eggs, right? Of course they do. You can use egg shapes to make bird drawings too.

Step 1
Draw an egg shape for the body.

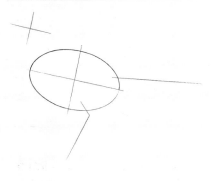

Step 3
Add some lines to join the head to the body.

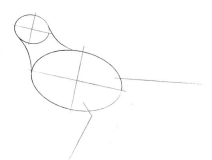

Step 2
Draw a smaller egg shape for the head. Have a think about how far the head needs to be from the body first. It might overlap the body.

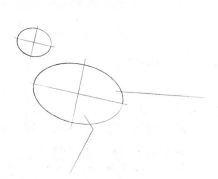

Step 4
Add the beak. Or it will get very hungry.

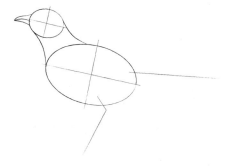

Step 5

Add an eye. Or it will fly into things. Take care to get the eye in the right place.

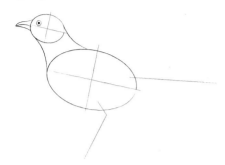

Step 6

Add the wing. Or it won't be able to fly! This is a sort of teardrop shape.

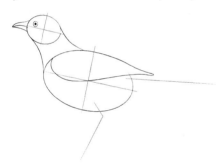

Step 7

Add a tail. That helps it steer.

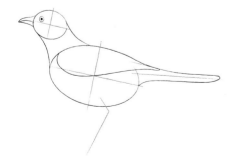

Step 8

Give it legs and feet. Most birds have three toes pointing to the front, and one to the back. You could search for pictures on the Internet to help you.

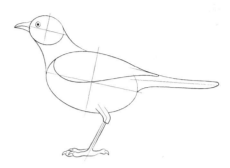

Step 9

Sit down and laugh at your picture. Actually, it might be quite good…

Try to draw while looking at real, live birds. Birds that squawk and flap and hop and poo. Drawing them makes you look at them closely. And that helps you get to know them better.

Make a collage bird

This is a fun way to create a birdy masterpiece.

Make your collage on card. It needs to be A4 (that's twice as big as this book) or bigger. Card will hold the bits better than paper and it won't flop around. Draw your bird shape onto the card. Or find a picture of a bird in a magazine or on the Internet and stick that on your card.

You'll need lots of bits to glue on to your bird shape. The box on page 27 gives you some ideas. There are lots of other things you could use too.

What type of post do pigeons carry?

Dove letters

THINGS TO STICK ON YOUR BIRD

- Torn up bits of old magazines or newspapers.
- Leaves. But don't pull them off living plants. They need them more than you do. Don't use them if there are minibeasts living on them.

- Buttons.
- Pipe cleaners.
- Sweet wrappers.
- Bits of used wrapping paper.
- Wobbly eyes.
- Feathers. Only if the birds left them behind somewhere.

You can make your bird look like a real bird, or you can make up a bird. If you make one up, give it a name. Not Bert or Sally. The 'long-billed worm-sucker' or something like that!

Pecking wood

Some birds are ace singers, but not all of them. The great spotted woodpecker doesn't even try to sing. It drums instead, and it doesn't need drumsticks. Check out the RSPB's website to hear one drumming – it's a great noise.

Have a go

Imagine you're a woodpecker. Put one hand near your mouth so that it sticks out like a beak. Hold your other hand in front of your face – that's the tree trunk.

Here's the challenge. Get someone to time you for five seconds. See how many times you can hit the tree trunk with your beak in five seconds.

No cheating! It's not the tree that moves, it's the beak. And the beak must stay attached to your head while you're pecking!

Now it's time for a bit of maths. Work out how many times you pecked the trunk in one second. To do that, divide your five second count by five.

Look out for colourful green woodpeckers in Britain too.

You were rubbish!

Guess what? You weren't anywhere near as fast as a real woodpecker! If you were really fast maybe you pecked four times in one second. Great spotted woodpeckers can peck at a speed of 18 pecks a second!

No headache

With all that head banging, why don't woodpeckers get headaches? To keep its brain intact a woodpecker needs some special protection. Scientists looked at the head of an American woodpecker. Some of its skull is spongy to stop the bird knocking its brains out!

Can you peck as fast as this great spotted woodpecker?

INTERESTING WOODPECKER STUFF

- Woodpeckers like drumming on dead wood. But some of them use the metal bits on telegraph poles instead!
- You can hear a drumming woodpecker about half a mile away.
- Listen for drumming between December and June.
- Single males drum more than paired ones. A male with no female might have 600 drumming sessions in one day. That's a lot of pecks! A male that has found a female drums 100–200 times a day.

Meet the family

10,400. That's a big number! It's roughly how many types – or species – of birds there are in the world. Birds come in different shapes, sizes and colours. Scientists have spent ages trying to work out how all the different types of birds are related to each other. They have organised them into groups of closely-related species. Each group is called a family. There are about 230 families of birds.

The Spotter's Guide in this book tells you about 25 different types of bird. These are birds you could see when you do the Big Schools' Birdwatch. You could see most of them in the Big Garden Birdwatch too. They can be grouped into families, like this:

Tits

Blue tit   Great tit   Coal tit

These are small birds that seem to be full of energy. Their main food is minibeasts. Look at the shape of a tit's beak – it's great for sticking into nooks and crannies and grabbing minibeasts. Tits nest in holes in trees and some of them use nestboxes. However, the long-tailed tit isn't a tit. It's in a totally different family – the bushtits. Impress your teacher with that!

Finches

Goldfinch   Greenfinch   Chaffinch

These finches all have 'finch' in their name. However, not all finches do. The siskin is a finch and so is the redpoll. Finches are small to medium-sized birds. They build their nests in trees and bushes, and most of them eat mainly seeds. Take a look at a finch's beak – it's more triangular than a tit's. Their beaks are made for scrunching seeds.

Goldfinch – a seed scruncher.

Crows
Carrion crow
Rook Jackdaw Magpie
These four crows look similar. Even the magpie looks like a crow if you take a good look at its head. Crows are medium to large, chunky birds. They eat lots of different things – seeds, fruit, minibeasts and bigger animals.

Jackdaw – a mostly black crow with a pale eye.

Pigeons
Woodpigeon Collared dove
Feral pigeon
You can see that these birds are related. Pigeons are medium to large birds. They have small heads, and mostly, they eat bits of plants. They are quite chunky though – some woodpigeons look like they need to go on a diet!

Gulls
Black-headed gull Common gull
Herring gull
Most gulls are big birds. They have webs between their toes. The adults are mainly grey, white and black. You can see them in a lot of places, not just at the seaside. But they do build their nests by the sea or near somewhere wet. They often nest close to lots of other gulls. This is called a breeding colony and it can be very noisy.

Thrushes and chats
Robin Blackbird Song thrush
This is a big group of small to medium-sized birds. The small ones, like the robin, are called 'chats'. The larger ones are 'true thrushes'. There are some great singers in this family – have a listen to the songs of these three for a start.

The other ones
Sparrows look like finches but they are in a different family – the sparrow family. Starlings are in the starling family and, guess what, wrens are in the wren family! The pied wagtail is in a group with other wagtails and streaky-brown birds called pipits.

That just leaves the dunnock. That's in a group called the accentors. It's the only member of its family that lives in this country.

Inventabird

A 'habitat' is the place where a plant or animal lives.

Real birds have all sorts of tricks to help them live in different types of habitats. For example, they might have different shaped beaks, different shaped bodies and different colours. They do different things too.

Now think of a funny habitat. It could be one of the bins in your school playground, the head teacher's office, the space behind the sofa, or the back of the frozen food cabinet at the supermarket. Come up with some ideas of your own too.

Next invent a bird that lives there. Think about:

- What it eats and how it finds or catches its food
- How it makes sure its enemies can't find it
- What it does to attract a mate
- Where and how it builds a nest

Make a picture of your bird, either on paper or on a computer. Give it a name. Label the picture to point out all the important bits. Find an audience and tell them how your bird lives. You will be the world expert on your bird!

Which bird lives in a fridge?
A coldfinch

Dawn chorus

The spring is the best time to hear the dawn chorus. It can be wonderfully noisy. Some birds start singing while it's still dark. As the sun comes up, more and more birds will be shouting out their songs. It's an amazing bird event and you really should try to hear it at least once a year.

It's great to get outside at dawn!

However, you have to start very early. April, May and June are all good dawn chorus months. To really soak up its sounds you need to be up by 4am or earlier! A patch of wood is a good place to go for your dawn chorus treat. If there are no woods nearby don't worry – you can hear birds singing in most places. You'll need a grown-up with you, so they have to get up too. You'll have to ask them very nicely. Try telling them that it's a wonderful wildlife experience that they shouldn't miss. Or bribe them with chocolate.

How to cheat

Don't bother getting up! Stay in bed with the window open to listen. Or you could do the dusk chorus instead. This is another burst of birdsong before birds go to bed. Fewer birds do it and it's spread out over a longer period, so it's not normally as amazing as the dawn show, but it's still pretty good. You might have to stay up a bit late but you won't have to get up early.

How do I know what's singing?

Unless you are good at bird song, there will be lots of noises you don't recognise. But so what? A singer still sounds as good even if you don't know their name. Just enjoy it! Then have your favourite breakfast and go back to bed.

Natural art

What do you call 10 ducks in a cardboard box?

A box of quackers

There's more to art than paint and pencils! Here's some cool art you can do outside. You won't need any special art kit.

You are going to create a work of art using bits of nature. It's a collage without glue. First, find a piece of ground to work on. It needs to be flat, and not too sloping – or your masterpiece will slide away! A bare patch in a wood is good, or somewhere on a nice, sandy beach.

Have a good look around to see what you could use to make your picture.

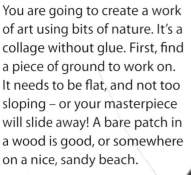

Why not use leaves to make feathers on a bird?

Please don't use plants or animals that are still alive – let them live! Take care not to take a creature's home for your masterpiece either. If there are animals living on anything you want to use, find something else.

You may already have an idea for your picture. Your favourite bird? Or another bit of wonderful wildlife? If you don't know, have a good look at the materials you could use. Do their colours and shapes remind you of any wildlife? That could be your picture. If you're still stuck create a design instead of a picture – something with great shapes and colours.

Then put the bits together to make your art. You could use a stick or stone to scratch some outlines on the ground if it helps. When it's done you could put a frame of sticks around it. Don't forget to wash your hands when you're done. Especially before you have your dinner.

If you can, take a photo of your work of art. The real thing won't last forever. Leave it where you made it and other people can enjoy it. It might make them want to do one too!

YOU COULD USE:

Leaves
Moss
Twigs and sticks
Stones and pebbles
Soil
Seeds
Fruits
Seashells

35

Act like a bird

Some birds do the same thing again and again. Wagtails wag their tails – that's an easy one. Watch a blackbird – it 'pumps' its tail when it lands. Some of these actions can help you work out what type of bird you are looking at. It's not just about what a bird looks like, it's about how it acts too!

Watch some birds first with your friends. Look for things that one type of bird does again and again. Then think about how you could act that out.

Now take it in turns to act like a bird. The people who are watching have to guess what kind of bird the actor is trying to be. If your acting is not very good, or the others can't work out what you are, this could go on for a very long time! You don't want to miss dinner, so you're only allowed 30 seconds to act. Then someone else has a go.

HOW ABOUT ACTING LIKE ONE OF THESE BIRDS?

- Pied wagtail – hold your arm behind you like a tail. Walk fast and wag your tail!
- Woodpigeon – have a go at their up and down display flight (see page 121).

- Starling – you'll need at least three of you to act this one, and you'll need to practice. Do some formation flying with wings out, flapping, twisting and turning at the same time. But don't bump into each other.

What do birds watch after the news?

The feather forecast

You could also use some simple props to help you. For example, a rolled-up newspaper for the wagtail's tail.

Come here birds!

You don't have to go to nature reserves to see birds. Think about what birds need to survive. Like you, they need to eat and drink. They also need somewhere to build a nest. They need places to sing from, a bit of shelter and somewhere to sleep. Give them as many of these things as you can, and the birds will come to you!

Different birds – different homes

The word for a place where an animal lives is 'habitat'. You know this next bit already – different birds live in different habitats. Puffins don't live in hedges and blackbirds don't swim on the sea. So if you want a variety of birds to come to you, you will have to give them different habitats. Some trees or bushes. A hedge maybe. Some grassy areas. Get the idea?

Get bird-brained

Imagine you're a bird flying over your school or garden. When a bird looks down it doesn't think 'that's Daniel's garden', or 'oh look, there's Kate's school'. They see lots of gardens all joined up into one big patch. To a bird, all those gardens might look like woodland, with bushes, grassy areas and a few ponds.

The countryside is not as bird-friendly as it used to be. So gardens are more important for wildlife than ever. Here's your challenge. Turn part of your school grounds or garden into your own nature reserve. You could even give it a name.

A sunflower. Wonderful colour, and then it's a natural bird feeder!

A good bath helps this starling look after its feathers.

What do I do?

Give them some food. This is easy, and it works. Take a look at pages 54–55 for some ideas. You could buy some proper bird feeders. Some feeders and bird foods that are sold are not very good. Try to buy ones recommended by a wildlife charity.

Give them a drink and a bath. No, you don't bathe them yourself, you just put out some water and let them do it. They don't even need a towel. There's more info on pages 56–57.

Give them a place to raise chicks. That's a nestbox. Check out pages 60–61 to find out how.

Do some gardening

Plant trees and bushes. Look at pages 8–9 for more information. There are other plants you could try too. How about growing sunflowers? They look good, and you can watch the birds eating the seeds straight from the sunflower. Plants that have leaves all year round (evergreens) and plants with sharp, spiky thorns (ouch) make good nest sites too.

Think food chain

Plant wildflowers and bushes that attract insects. You'll be helping the insects, and because some birds eat them, you'll be helping birds too.

The bigger birdwatch

When you've done all this, you'll see even more birds when you do the Big Schools' Birdwatch or Big Garden Birdwatch. So what are you waiting for?

Design your own game

Here are some ideas:

That's my food!

Give each player a list of different things birds eat. The list could include fish, voles, worms, seeds and caterpillars. Read out a bird's name. The first player to stick their hand up is allowed to answer, with the name of a food eaten by that bird. If they get it right they get a point. If they get it wrong they lose a point. Then someone else has a go. You'll have to do a bit of work to find out what birds eat those foods. Use the Spotter's Guide in this book to help you.

I'm out of here!

This is about migration. Find out about a bird that is only here in the summer. Where does it go in the winter? Which countries does it travel through to get there? Which seas does it fly over? What dangers does it face?

Now make a board game to tell the story. A storm might send your bird back three squares. Or something might eat it and send it back ten squares. Then again, the wind might be behind it so it might leap on five squares.

Create your own game to help you find out more about birds!

Migration is a great subject for a game.

If you're making a board game, you might find pictures you can use in old magazines or online. If you're searching on the computer, tell a grown-up what you're up to.

So now, when someone says 'time for homework', you just have to say that you're learning serious things about ornithology, which is the study of birds. But you'll have to practice saying the 'orni' word first.

MORE IDEAS

- Beaks and feet: can you stick them on the right body?
- Which bird goes with which food?
- Which noise goes with which bird? (There are lots of bird noises on the RSPB website to help you.)
- Mixed-up names: jumble up the letters in different bird names.
- Pin the tail on the Pintail. (Yes, that is a real bird. It's a type of duck).

Feather-free fun

Birds are great. But there are lots of other animals that are just as amazing. Minibeasts are some of the easiest ones to find. Here's how.

Look at the flowers

Insects like flowers. Watch some flowers for a while, especially if it's sunny, and you will probably see some insects. If you see something that looks a bit like a wasp and bit like a fly, it's a hoverfly. It hovers but it doesn't sting. It's a lot less bother than a wasp! There are loads of different hoverflies. Most of them love drinking nectar. Then there are bees, butterflies, moths and more. Some moths come out in the day as well as the night.

Find a pond

Take a good look at a pond (you'll need a grown-up with you). There will be beasts on the water, under the water, around the edges of the water and maybe over the water. Try to work out what they are by looking them up.

Lots of hoverflies look like wasps or bees.

Look under logs, rocks and bricks

But do it carefully. They can be heavy and you don't want to squash your fingers or the minibeasts. You might need a grown-up to help. These are great places to find beetles, slugs, centipedes, millipedes and woodlice. Put the logs or rocks back gently when you've finished. If you caught any beasts for a closer look, let them go at the side of the log or rock. They will find their own way back under.

Ponds are good places to look for damselflies.

Just look!

Walk slowly and look carefully. Check leaves, grass, stems, branches and bushes. Because you are shorter than the grown-ups you will spot things that they miss!

Whack a branch

Here's something that scientists do. Get an old sheet and spread it under a low branch of a bush or tree. Then use a stick to give the branch a sharp knock. If it works, any minibeasts on the branch won't have time to hold on so they will fall down onto the sheet for you to look at.

Make your own bird guide

This will help you learn your birds! And you'll have a book that you can use that you wrote yourself.

You probably want to do some other things before you get old so don't try to write too big a book. Try doing a guide to ten common birds you can see in your school grounds or your garden.

First choose your birds. Then spend some time watching them. Get to know them. Then you can sound like an expert when you do the writing. In fact, if you spend some time watching them you might become an expert.

Make a list of things to include about each bird. These can be the headings that you use. They will help you organise your book. You might have one heading for size, one for what it looks like and one for where you normally see them. Try to put in some facts about how they live too. Where do they build their nest? How many eggs do they lay?

There are two ways to find your facts. Some things you will be able to see for yourself – which trees the birds use for example. But you won't find all the facts that way. You might notice that a bird isn't here in the winter. You won't know where it's gone but could look in a book or on the Internet to find out. You can find lots of other facts there too. The RSPB or the BTO website are good places to start.

What you put in is up to you. Think up your own headings and make it your book. Put in the stuff that helps you and that you think is interesting. You don't want to be bored by your own book!

You'll need pictures and words for your book. Do the work on a computer. The words will look tidy and they will take up less space. You may be able to find some pictures on the computer too. Or cut them out of magazines and stick them on later.

When it's done, print it out. If you cut it to A5 (about the size of this book) it will be easy to put in a bag. Make a cover for it and print this on card. You might need a grown-up to help you get all the pages in the right order. If you're a computer whiz, they might need you to show them! To hold the pages together you'll need a stapler with a long arm. There should be one of these at school.

Guess what? You've just written a book.

What did the mother jackdaw say to the baby jackdaw?
Flap jack, flap jack

Words about birds

Do you like playing with words? If you do, why not…

…pen a poem?
This one is about the cuckoo.

I saw him flying in the sky,
In a flash he passed me by,
He didn't know he'd grown in my tum,
If only he knew that I was his mum.

See if you can do better.

…laugh at a limerick?

Limericks have five lines. Lines one, two and five rhyme with each other. So do lines three and four. Here's one about a collared dove.

There was a fat dove called Bess,
Whose nest was a horrible mess,
She laid her eggs in a flash,
One fell through with a crash,
And then there was one egg less!

Find the words that rhyme first. Then write the rest of your limerick. Make it funny.

I'm famous. Someone has written a poem about me.

...assemble an acrostic?

This means writing something where the first letters of each line spell a word. If it was about a small brown bird with a sticky-up tail it could go something like this:

Wild singer
Round in shape
Ever so small
Notice my tail

What did the little bird say to the big bird?
Peck on someone your own size

Sometimes robins can be a bit fierce!

If you want to have a go at an acrostic, start with birds with short names! You could try swan, heron, coot, owl, crow, rook or jay. Or robin...

Red
Orange
Breast, but
I'm
Not always nice!

Now you have a go.

Be an explorer!

Imagine going somewhere no one else has ever been. You're in a team of explorers. You don't know what you will find. It's a strange land. There are some plants and animals that you know about. But some of them are not in any books! There could be beautiful creatures, scary creatures, and strange creatures. Some of the plants could be cures for horrible diseases.

You are going to explore a wonderful place that you've made up in your head! When you get back you have to tell other scientists about it.

Where do tough birds come from?
Hard-boiled eggs

Could a toucan live there?

THINK ABOUT...

- How did you get there? Did you walk, fly, crawl through tunnels...
- What was the weather like? It could be like no weather anywhere else.
- What did it look like? Hilly? Flat? What colours were there? Were there rivers or lakes? Trees? Deserts?
- What plants were there?
- What animals were there?
- What should this new land be called?
- What needs to be done to protect it?

Wow! What wonderful land will you explore?

Work out what you want to say. Use words and pictures to tell your story. You can draw the pictures or make them on a computer. You could use the computer to change photos of real animals to make them look like the new creatures you found. Why not draw a map of your imaginary land? Make sure you put all the main things you saw on the map and give them names.

Do this activity with some friends if you like. They could be experts on different things, such as birds, plants or insects. Some of your other friends could explore different places and speak about them.

Then tell your friends or the rest of your class about it. They are the group of other scientists. When you have told your story, you answer their questions.

Have fun exploring. But make sure you get back safely!

Feather facts

What is it that makes a bird a bird? It's not that they can fly. Bats, butterflies and beetles can do that too – and some birds can't. It's feathers. No other animal has feathers.

What are feathers made of?

The main ingredient of feathers is keratin. It's a type of protein. Your hair and toenails have keratin in them too. Feathers don't weigh much – they are as light as… feathers.

How many feathers do birds have?

It depends on the bird. Swans have lots. Someone once counted the feathers on a swan and there were over 25,000. Not all birds are this feathery. 940 feathers were counted on a ruby-throated hummingbird. You won't see one of those in this country though. However, you might see a house sparrow – their feathers have been counted too! How many do you think there were? (the answer is at the bottom of the opposite page).

Types of feather

Contour feathers. These are the small ones that cover the bird's body. They overlap each other like tiles on a roof. This gives the bird a smooth shape and that makes flying easier. It protects them from the wind and rain too.

Down feathers. These are the bird's underwear! They wear them like a vest under their other feathers to keep warm. Down feathers are small and soft.

Flight feathers. These are the big feathers in the wings and tail. They are the strong feathers that are used for flying.

Feathers are amazing and only birds have them.

Mandarin ducks are dressed for showing off!

What else are feathers used for?

To help birds hide. The colours of some feathers make it very easy for their owner to hide. Being good at hiding means you might not get eaten!

To show off. Some male birds use their colours to impress the females. If they impress a female enough they can mate with her. Colours can say something different to another male though. A robin's red-orange breast helps it find a mate, but is also used to tell another male to 'get out of here'.

Show-off or hide? Look at some ducks. The males and females usually look very different. The male is the show-off. The female has feathers that help her hide. When she is sitting on her eggs, it helps to hide the nest.

Feather care

Birds look after their feathers by preening. Normally they use their beak to help 'zip up' any gaps. Try this yourself when you find a feather. Lots of birds spread a special oil on their feathers too. This is made near the tail. It helps to keep the water out.

House sparrow answer: 3000–3500.

Become a species expert

Lots of bird watchers are good at knowing the names of different birds. But some of them don't know much about birds! It's like knowing your friend's name but not knowing what they like to do.

What says quick, quick?
A duck with hiccups

Birds using nestboxes are good ones to study.

We're going to turn you into a species expert. Scientists talk about 'species' not 'types' of bird. A blue tit is one species and a great tit is another species.

Going expert

First, pick a bird that you want to know more about. Pick one that you can see easily in the wild. One that you can watch out of the window would be good.

Now you know what you're going to be an expert on. To be an expert you don't have to wear wellies and grow a big bushy beard. Especially if you're a girl.

Experts know things. So you need to find things to know. Look for facts in books and on the Internet. Try 'Birds by name' on the RSPB website, and 'Birdfacts' on the BTO website. You could also use the Spotter's Guide in this book to help you.

- What are they eating?
- Where do you see them?
- Are they on their own or in a flock?

If there are birds using a nestbox you could study them.

- When did they first go in?
- What did they bring to build the nest?
- When could you hear chicks calling?
- What did the parents feed them on?
- How often did they visit?
- When did the baby birds come out?

But don't stop there! Watch the birds yourself. There are loads of questions you can ask. Seeing things yourself is a great way of learning. You might see something that no one else has ever seen!

To really look expert, ask your teacher if you can give a talk about your bird at school.

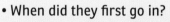

Which bird never gets food stuck in its throat?

A swallow

With a bit of work you could become a house sparrow expert.

Make your own bird feeder

Here is an easy way to make bird feeders out of rubbish. You'll need a cardboard fruit juice carton, like the one in the picture. The first thing to do is drink all the juice. Then rinse the carton with water and let it dry. Don't throw the lid away. If you do, your feeder will have a hole in the roof.

Making the feeder is easy

Use a hole punch to make two holes in the bit that sticks up at the top.

Reusing is better than recycling.

Make some small holes in the bottom so that water can drain out. You might need a grown-up to help with this.

Cut a hole in one or two sides of the carton with scissors. If you make holes in two sides, do opposite ones. Cut along three sides of a rectangle.

Fold the card out and cut most of it off. Leave a bit sticking out to protect the seeds.

Use wire or string to make a loop on the top.

Put in some bird seed and hang it up.

You can make feeders from plastic bottles too.

SOME OTHER TREATS FOR THE BIRDS

- Bread – but not huge pieces.
- Crumbs from your lunch box – bread crumbs, biscuit crumbs, cake crumbs, but not crisps.
- Fruit – apples and pears that fell off the tree are good.
- Porridge oats – but don't cook them! Birds like their porridge raw.
- Raw pastry.
- Boiled rice – unless it has salt in it. Salt isn't good for birds.
- Potatoes – baked or boiled, but not salted.

NOT JUST FOOD

Birds also need things to build their nests with. You can give them some. Funny things turn up in birds' nests. Guess what has been found in red kites' nests? Socks. And pants! But don't leave your pants out for the birds. You need them. When you have your hair cut, let the birds have that.

When you brush your dog, give the birds the fur. Leave it in small piles on the ground. Then watch and see who takes it.

You could also try straw, grass, twigs and leaves. It's best to do this at the start of spring.

Water for wildlife

Water is good for you. It's good for birds too. They drink it and they wash in it, just like you do. Make their lives easier by giving them some water.

Find a flowerpot tray that's about 20cm across or bigger. Clean it up, pop a stone in the middle to weigh it down and stop birds bathing in it. Then pour in some water. Easy!

Or find the lid of an old rubbish bin that isn't needed any more. Give it a clean and turn it upside down.

CLEANING THE BATH

Look after your birdbath. Keep it topped up with water. Give it a clean sometimes – don't let it get mucky!

It will wobble. To stop it wobbling, put some bricks or stones under the edges or dig a hole to put it in. Put a rock or a brick in the middle. You can put some other rocks or bits of brick in too. Then just add water.

Put your birdbath where you can see what the birds get up to. Make sure cats can't grab them though – don't put the bath too near to bushes or trees that a cat could hide in. You could put lots of spiky plant cuttings under any bushes to keep cats away too.

Birds need water too!

Your birdbath could attract frogs too.

Frogbath

It's not just birds that might use this new watery place. You might find frogs in it or midge larvae wriggling in the water. To make a simple frog hut turn a clay flowerpot upside-down. Use a broken pot – one with a bit missing from the edge. Then the frogs can get in and out.

ICE IN THE BATH

In the winter your birdbath could freeze. A small, floating ball helps to stop it icing over. If it does freeze up, add some hot water to melt it. Who wants a cold bath anyway?! Don't put salt in the water to stop it freezing.

Mega-journeys

Imagine you're a swallow. It's the summer and you've got a nest in Britain. You love eating insects and there are plenty around. You have five hungry chicks to feed. To keep them happy you feed them about 6000 insects every day. It doesn't get dark until late in the evening, so you can spend lots of time bringing them food.

A redwing – one of our winter guests.

In a few months' time it will be winter. There won't be many insects around. So what do you do? You get out of here before it's too late! In the autumn, you start a long journey and fly to South Africa. There are loads of insects there. Then you fly back to Britain to breed here again next summer. This mega-journey to Africa and back is called 'migration'.

Here for the summer

Some birds come to Britain for the summer. Swallows, swifts, house martins and cuckoos are good examples. Most of our summer visitors go to Africa for the winter.

Here for the winter

This might surprise you. There are some birds that come to Britain for the winter. These include swans, geese, ducks, and types of thrushes called redwings and fieldfares. Most of our winter visitors come to us from the really cold bits of Europe, Iceland and Greenland.

Not stopping

Some migrating birds stop here for a while on their way to somewhere else. They don't breed here or spend the winter here. They just stop for a rest and some food before moving on.

No map needed!

You probably know your way to school. But what if you had to find your way to Africa on your own? And you had never done it before?

Somehow, migrating birds know they have to fly in a certain direction. Natural clues help them find their way. They can use the sun or stars as a compass. The sun and stars are in different places at different times, so a migrating bird needs a clock too. It doesn't wear a watch, but there is something inside it that works like a clock.

Birds that migrate at night can use the place where the sun went down to help them find their way. Birds even use the earth's magnetic fields to help them. That must be good if it's too cloudy to see the stars. Just like you, they spot things they know. They might follow a river to help them find their way. And when they are nearly there, some birds use smell to get to the right spot! Many mega-journey birds use more than one of these tools to find their way.

Let's get fat

You need plenty of fuel for a long journey. For a bird, this means fat. Before they leave, birds eat and eat and eat. Minibeasts and berries are good migration fuel. Sedge warblers are small, brown birds. They stuff their beaks with aphids before they fly to Africa. They eat so much that their weight doubles! Then they fly 4000km without stopping. It takes about three or four days.

Take a rest

Not all birds fly non-stop. Most do the journey bit by bit. They can stop, have a rest, eat and then carry on. They might stop for weeks before heading off again.

Swallows are famous mega-journey birds.

Build a nestbox

A nestbox is a box pretending to be a hole in a tree. Blue tits and great tits often nest in nestboxes. Especially if there aren't many trees with holes in!

You will need a grown-up to help you with this. You need wood and tools.

Search for 'nestbox' on the RSPB website. Your box doesn't have to be exactly this size – the birds won't check it with a ruler!

Don't forget to make some holes in the floor of the box. Then if any water does get in, it can get out too! To help keep your baby birds safe, make sure the hole on the front is 12.5cm (or more) up off the floor. That makes it hard for cats to take birds out.

You'll need a hinge for the lid. Go to the bike shop and ask for a bit of old inner tube. Cut it up and use that. You don't need to paint your box with anything.

You can help birds by putting up nestboxes.

WHAT SIZE HOLE?

It depends what birds you want. Big birds can't get in small holes. Small birds can go through bigger holes though.

Diameter of hole (how many millimetres across)	What birds does it work for?
25mm	Blue tit. Coal tit
28mm	Great tit
32mm	House sparrow

A big square hole

Some birds use boxes with half the front missing! Make the bit of wood on the front only 10–14cm high. Now you've made a box for wrens, robins or pied wagtails.

Where do I put it?

If your box has a hole in it, put it on a tree or wall. It should be two to four metres off the ground. Don't put it in bright sunshine or where rain can blow in through the hole. You can use wire to fix your box to a tree. If you have made a box for house sparrows ask a grown-up to put it on a wall just below the roof.

If your box has half its front missing you need to hide it low down (less than two metres up) in lots of plant cover. A wall covered in ivy would be a great place for a nestbox like this.

Spring clean?

Do an autumn clean instead. Make sure the birds have finished using the box first! Don't do it before August. Take out the old nest. Scrape out any other bits and pieces. Then pour hot water into the box and let it dry. Make sure you wash your hands afterwards!

Box cameras

Time to talk nicely to the grown-ups again. You can buy nestboxes with cameras in them. You can also buy cameras to put in nestboxes. If you get one of those, you can watch the birds inside your box.

Computer art

If you're stuck inside and want to do something birdy, you could do it on the computer.

Digital posters

Find some pictures of birds, places where birds live or anything else to do with birds. They could be pictures you've taken with a phone or camera. You might find pictures on the Internet that you can use. If you can't find anything on the computer, scan pictures from magazines or some of your own drawings. Then use the computer to stick lots of pictures together to make one big, wild poster.

If you want to use some words too think of these before you find the pictures. Then you can find pictures that go with the words.

WORDS FOR BIRDS

How about...

- Feed the birds
- Birds need water
- Homeless! Please help (*put up a nestbox for house sparrows*)
- Wanted – home for young family (*put up a nestbox*)
- Mum and Dad know best (*leave baby birds alone*)

Or think up your own words.

Why not scan or photograph a picture that you've drawn or painted? Then use the computer to stick this picture onto another picture. You could draw a bird and then stick it on a photo of a tree. Or on a feeder. Or on your friend's head…

Another idea

Make your poster or picture the old-fashioned way. Cut bits out and stick them on to a piece of A4 paper. You can write on the paper too. Then scan it, and save it on the computer. Make sure the glue is dry before you put the paper in the scanner! You can print lots of copies from the computer. You could even make cards to send to your friends.

Judge: *"Do you have anything to say?"*
Owl: **"No I don't give a hoot"**

The bare bits – beaks and feet

Birds have bare bits. They don't have feathers everywhere. Their beaks are bare, and on most birds, their feet and legs are too. These bare parts give you clues about how a bird lives.

Basic beak speak

A beak is a tool that birds use for eating. The shape and size of a beak tells you something about what a bird eats and how it finds its food. Take a look at a sparrow's beak or a finch's. Now look at the beak on a blue tit or great tit. They are different. Sparrows and finches have beaks that look more like a triangle – they are seed crunchers. The tits have more pointy beaks – these are for grabbing insects and other minibeasts.

Rip it up

Kestrels, sparrowhawks and other birds of prey have strong hooked beaks with knife-like edges. They use them to cut and rip up their meaty meals. Yum.

Water filters

Some ducks are filter feeders. Imagine toothbrush bristles around the edge of a duck's beak. Water can get out, but small animals get stuck. Then they get eaten. That's how a filter feeder's beak works.

Gone fishing

Herons and kingfishers use their long, sharp beaks to catch fish. Herons grab or stab their prey. Kingfishers usually grab.

Watch out fish!

Stick in the mud

Some birds, like the curlew, have long beaks. It sticks it in the mud to find worms, crabs and shellfish. Here's the clever bit. It can feel what it's doing with the tip of its beak. And it can open the tip of the beak without opening the rest of it.

Wood-pecking

Great spotted woodpeckers have strong, pointed beaks. They use them to find insects on bark and by pecking out holes in rotting wood. A very long, sticky tongue is also part of their feeding kit.

Let's talk about feet

Most birds have three toes pointing to the front and one pointing backwards. This works really well for birds that perch. Once they have landed, the feet automatically wrap themselves around the perch. But not all feet are like this…

Swimming feet

Ducks, geese and swans have webs between their toes to help them swim. Gulls have webbed feet too. But not all swimming birds do. Coots have flaps along their toes to make swimming easier. When you see a coot walking, have a look at its feet.

Legs for wading

The long legs of herons and waders help to keep their feathers dry when they are walking in the water.

Killing feet

The feet of a bird of prey are strong and have sharp talons. They use them to grab and hold on to their prey. The pads on the toes give them a good grip. Most birds of prey kill with their feet too.

Tell a wild story

But it has to be true. You can't make it up. You'll need wildlife facts, and you have to find them. Don't look for them in books or on the computer. Look for them in the wild.

First, find somewhere wild. Forget big mountains and crocodile swamps. Find somewhere you can get to easily. Somewhere you like going. Somewhere that's safe for you to go. But not the shops or the pizza place! Somewhere a bit wild. The nature area in the school grounds or your back garden would be good.

Then study it. Start by exploring it. Use your senses – look, listen, touch and smell. Draw a map of your wild place, showing all the important bits. Decide how long your study will last. You can do it at any time of the year but spring is a good time to do it. There's lots of wild stuff going on then. Birds are singing and building nests. Leaves pop open on trees. Plants are growing again after their winter rest. If you really enjoy it, you can keep going for longer.

There will be lots of things you could include in your wild story. It could be huge! So that it's not too big, choose a few things to look at closely.

What do you call a wagtail in pastry?
A pied wagtail

FACT-FINDING

Here are some ideas to get you started:

Birds
- What birds are there?
- Where do you see them?
- When do you see them?
- What are they doing?
- Why are they doing it?

Minibeasts
- What minibeasts can you find?
- Where are they?
- Why do you think they are there and not somewhere else?
- What do you think they eat?

Plants
- When do the leaves pop open on different trees?
- When do different flowers open up?

Take your time. Ask questions. See if you can work out the answers. You can use books to work out what things are, and to help you work out what's going on. But trust what you see yourself too.

Write it down

There could be different sections for different bits – one for birds, one for minibeasts and one for plants. Or you could write a diary. You can also add drawings and paintings. Use a phone or camera to take some photos. You can put those in too. There may be some nature you can stick in like feathers. Try to work out what bird they came from and why they are not on the bird any more. Or maybe some leaves. But don't pull them off living plants and check that there are no minibeasts living on them. You could do some of it on a computer if you like.

Tell your wild story the way you want to tell it. Have fun!

67

Be an ornithologist

An orni-what? This means someone who studies birds – a scientific bird watcher. Ornithologists don't just know the names of birds. They discover things about how they live too and record the results. Now it's your turn to try a bit of ornithology.

Who eats what?

Fill some bird feeders with bird food. You could try a seed mix, such as sunflower seeds, nyjer seeds and peanuts. Put the feeders where you can see them. You are going to find out if the birds have a favourite feeding spot. Every time you see a bird at the feeders, write down what it is eating and where. The longer you do this for the more information you will collect. Draw a table to help you.

Which one is the boss?

Watch what the birds do at your feeders or bird table. Some birds don't like sharing the food. They drive other birds away. Find out who the bullies are! Make a table to show this. Every time you see a bird drive another one away make a mark in the right box on the table.

> What is a bird's favourite biscuit?
> *A chocolate chirp cookie*

Who's the boss of the garden?

A bit of science can make your bird watching even more rewarding.

Territory maps

This is something you can do when birds are singing. One of the reasons birds sing is to make sure that no other birds breed in the same area. They do this to make sure there is enough food for their family. These areas are called breeding territories.

Draw a map of your school grounds. To make your territory map, you need to see a bird singing so that you know what it is. Start with one type of bird. Every time you hear it sing, make a mark on the map to show where it sang from. If you think there is more than one bird singing, use different colours for different birds. Do this every day for two weeks.

Then have a good look at the marks on the map. Join up the marks around the edge that are in the same colour. That gives you a rough idea of that bird's territory. Remember, some of its territory could be outside the school ground.

Here are the answers!

But what are the questions? Well, they are ones that lots of people ask about birds.

How can I stop birds flying into my window?

Glass is usually see-through, so birds might not realise it is there. That's why they fly into it. Help them to avoid it by sticking pictures of birds on the outside of the window. There are special stickers you can buy, or you can make your own. You could also put some sticky plastic shapes on the window. Whatever you stick on your window, it will help birds to see there is glass there. Make sure you have a grown-up's permission before you start sticking things though.

I've found a baby bird. What do I do?

The best thing you can do is nothing! Leave it alone. Most garden birds scramble out of the nest before they can fly. It might be two more days before they take to the air. But the grown-up birds look after them. And they are better at it than you are! Their Mum or Dad may be watching them, or may be out getting some food. If the baby bird is somewhere dangerous, move it somewhere safe, but don't move it very far. The parents need to be able to find it again.

A young blackbird. Leave it alone!

I've found an injured bird. What do I do?

Often all you need to do is put a bird in a box somewhere dark and quiet. Leave it there for a bit, and the bird might feel better. Then you can just let it go. If it needs more help, take it to a vet or call the RSPCA.

We have an old egg collection. Can we keep it?

Sorry, you can't. You might not believe it, but some people steal eggs from nests. These people are criminals. It's against the law to keep wild birds' eggs or sell them. See if a museum would like the eggs. If they don't want them, the eggs should be smashed up and thrown away. Put the bits on the compost heap.

Our house martins have flown off to Africa. Should I knock their nest down before they come back?

If you went on a long holiday would you want your home knocked down while you were away? Leave it there. When they get back next spring they will move in again.

I've found some dead birds in my garden. Is my bird food killing them?

Probably not. But keep your bird table and feeders clean. If you keep finding dead birds, call the RSPB.

Song thrush eggs. Don't take them – it's against the law.

Put your foot in it!

A good wildlife detective spots all sorts of wild clues. Footprints tell you that an animal was there, even if you can't see it. Look for footprints in soft, wet mud and snow. Check piles of squidgy cow poo too – there might be bird footprints in those!

When you find a footprint, you can draw it or take a photo. Or you can make a life-size 3D model to take home and keep. This is how you do it.

How to make a footprint plaster cast

Put a 'wall' around the footprint. This could be a circle made out of a strip of card held together with a paperclip. Another way to make the wall is cut the bottom off a plastic pot to make a short tube. Make the wall about 3cm higher than the track. Push the wall into the mud. Make sure there are no gaps around the edges.

Now you need a mixing pot. Put some water in it. Then add plaster of Paris and mix it up. Keep going until it looks like pouring cream.

Pour the plaster over the footprint. It should come up to near the top of the wall. There might be bubbles in the plaster. Tap the wall to get them out.

Then wait for it to dry. This could take up to an hour.

This gull is leaving some great footprints in the sand.

What is the only way out of an egg?
The egg-xit

Pick it up carefully. Brush off any dirt. Be gentle – you don't want to break your cast. Wrap it up in newspaper to protect it. Take it home. Leave it alone for a day or two. Then it will dry completely. If it needs a clean after that, put it under a tap and use a small brush.

Don't try this in snow. The plaster melts the footprint so it won't work.

If you know what bird or mammal made the footprint write it on the bottom of the cast. Write where and when you found it too. You can make the footprint easier to see by painting it black.

There are a few footprints here. These might help you work out what you saw.

Make a journey stick

Here's something you can do when you go for a walk somewhere that's a bit wild.

You need a strong stick about 30 to 40 cm long. Long sticks are good for long walks! Tie a small ball of wool or string to one end of the stick. Make sure you tie it on tightly so it doesn't fall off.

Now start walking. Look for natural things to collect that remind you of different bits of the walk – a leaf, a feather, a twig… When you collect something, wrap the wool or string around it to hold it on the stick. Don't cover it up, just wrap enough around it to hold it on. Attach the next thing you collect a bit further up the stick.

When you finish, your stick will have lots of things on it that remind you of where you've been and what you saw.

If you have some string, you can make a journey stick.

Spotter's Guide

The following pages look at 25 Big Birdwatch birds. Most of the birds that you will see when you do your birdwatch are here. This guide will help you work out which birds you see. Here's what you'll find for each bird.

The name

How big is it?

It might say something like 'sparrow-sized'. When you see a live bird you won't be able to measure it with a ruler. We've used sparrows and pigeons (feral pigeons or collared doves) to give you an idea of how big something is. Then we've told you how long the bird is, in centimetres. Imagine a bird lying flat on its back. Its length is the distance from the tip of its beak to the end of its tail.

What's it like?

These are a few describing words to help you get to know the bird.

What colour is it?

This tells you the main colours and markings.

What does it do?

Here you can find out some of the things this bird does. There are some tips to help you see some of the birds as well.

What noise does it make?

This tells you about some of the noises the bird makes. It's very hard to do this with words. Look at 'Birds by name' on the RSPB website. You can listen to recordings of their sounds here.

TOP TIP

Look out for the Top Tips. These will give you ideas about how to see a type of bird or work out what type of bird you're looking at.

It's a bit different in the summer

The birds on these pages are birds that you could see in the winter. Most of them can be seen in the summer too. There are also some extra birds you could see in the summer. You can find out more about some of them on pages 22–23.

Goldfinch

A red and yellow beauty.

How big is it?
A bit smaller than a sparrow.
A goldfinch is 12cm long.

What's it like?
Delicate, fluttery and colourful.

What colour is it?
Look for its red face and a yellow stripe
on each wing. Males and females look the
same. Young goldfinches don't have a red
face, but have the same sandy body colour.

What does it do?
A goldfinch is a brilliant seed-eater.
Look for it feeding on thistle and teasel
seeds. It takes seeds from bird feeders too.
A goldfinch flies in a bouncy line, going
up and down. In the autumn and winter
it can be seen in flocks. A goldfinch flock
provides wonderful flashes of colour.

What noise does it make?
A goldfinch song is tinkling and buzzy.
Its calls are tinkly too.

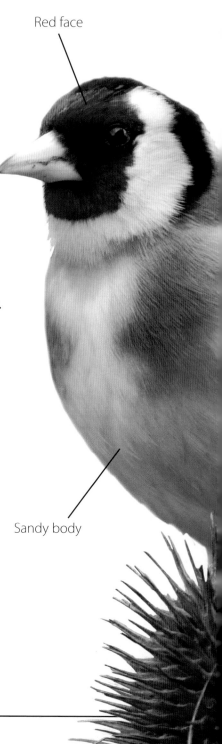

Red face

Sandy body

CARRY ON FEEDING

People used to catch goldfinches and keep them in cages, because they looked and sounded so good. One of the first things the RSPB did was to protect the goldfinch. There are now more goldfinches than there used to be in our gardens. This could be because we have been feeding them. Keep up the good work!

Yellow stripe on wing

TOP TIP

To attract goldfinches, put out some nyjer seed. These seeds are tiny. You'll need to put them in a special feeder with very small holes. If you use a normal feeder all the seeds will fall out. The small holes stop most of the other birds stealing the seeds too!

Greenfinch

The green seed-cruncher.

How big is it?
It's the size of a sparrow.
A greenfinch is 15cm long.

What's it like?
Chunky and green with a
tough looking beak.

What colour is it?
The male is mostly green with flashes
of yellow on his wings and tail. The
female looks like a very faded male.
She is more of a brown finch than a
greenfinch! But she does have some
yellow on her wings and tail.

TROUBLE FOR THE SEED-CRUNCHER

Some greenfinches have
died from a disease called
trichomonosis (try-ko-mon-
o-sis). They catch it from
pigeons. In the wild, pigeons
and greenfinches wouldn't
usually eat in the same
places. Keep your bird table
and feeders clean. That will
help the birds that eat there
stay healthy.

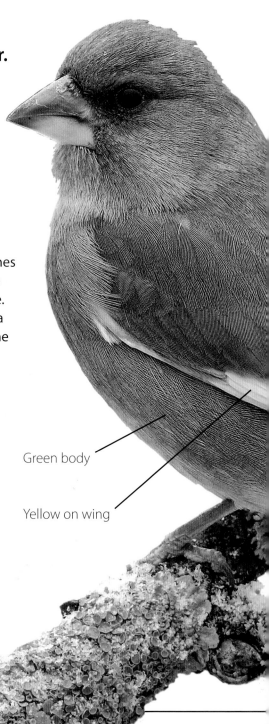

Green body

Yellow on wing

What does it do?

Takes lots of food from bird feeders. The greenfinch likes seeds, especially black sunflower ones. It's a messy eater! It gets the tasty bit out of the seed and leaves piles of seed cases under the feeder. It's a bit of a bully too – it doesn't like other birds coming to the feeder.

What noise does it make?

Its song is quite loud and rattly. It makes a stretched-out, wheezy noise too.

Yellow on tail

OLD GREENFINCH

It's unusual for a greenfinch to live for more than two years. But one old bird lived to see its 12th birthday! Scientists knew this because they had put a metal ring on its leg years before.

Chaffinch

Pretty in pink.

How big is it?

It's a little slimmer than a greenfinch.
A chaffinch is 14cm long.

What's it like?

The female looks like a sparrow, but with
lots of white on her wings. The male is
much more colourful, but still has
lots of white on his wings.

Blue-grey head

White patch
on shoulder

TOP TIP

You will often see flocks of
chaffinches that contain only male
birds. Look out for these brightly
coloured flocks. There may be
other small birds in the flocks as
well. See if you can spot any!

Pinkish front

What colour is it?

The male has a pinkish front and is dull green at the bottom of his back, near the tail. The top and back of his head is blue-grey. Check his wing for a white 'T' and a white patch on the shoulder. Look for white down the sides of his tail too. The female looks like a brown version of the male.

What does it do?

The chaffinch is a minibeast-muncher in the breeding season and a seed-scoffer the rest of the time. Most of the time it walks around on the ground looking for food, but it doesn't mind coming onto bird tables and bird feeders for an easy meal.

What noise does it make?

A chaffinch's song is musical and loud. The male can be easy to see when he is singing. He often perches somewhere high up and sings like a star! Chaffinches make a 'pink pink' call too. Take care – great tits make a noise that sounds just like it.

DIFFERENT VOICES

Just like people, chaffinches in different parts of the country sound different. They still sing a chaffinch song, but they sing it with different accents! Another noise the chaffinch makes is a buzzing call. This is its 'rain call'. If you hear it, watch to see if it rains.

House sparrow

Brown, streaky and cheeky!

How big is it?
Sparrow-sized of course!
A house sparrow is 14cm long.

What's it like?
Quite tough-looking
but friendly. It can be
very tame.

What colour is it?
The male is streaky brown
on the top, with grey
near the tail. He is greyish
underneath. Look for the
grey patch on the top of his
head, and his black bib. The
female is plainer, but still
streaky on top and greyish
below. She has a pale stripe
behind the eye and no bib.

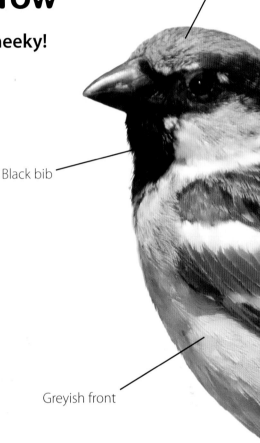

Grey patch

Black bib

Greyish front

TOP BIRD!

House sparrows keep getting to the top
of the Big Garden Birdwatch list. From
2004–2011, this little bird held on to the
number one spot. It is the bird that people
were seeing most, even though there are
not as many around as there used to be.
The starling was number one until the
house sparrow knocked it off its perch.

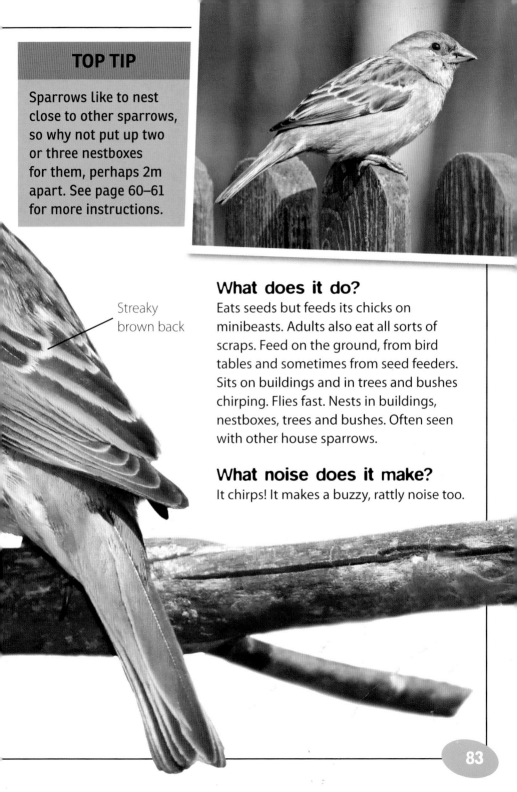

TOP TIP

Sparrows like to nest close to other sparrows, so why not put up two or three nestboxes for them, perhaps 2m apart. See page 60–61 for more instructions.

Streaky brown back

What does it do?

Eats seeds but feeds its chicks on minibeasts. Adults also eat all sorts of scraps. Feed on the ground, from bird tables and sometimes from seed feeders. Sits on buildings and in trees and bushes chirping. Flies fast. Nests in buildings, nestboxes, trees and bushes. Often seen with other house sparrows.

What noise does it make?

It chirps! It makes a buzzy, rattly noise too.

83

Dunnock

A bird that moves like a mouse.

How big is it?
Sparrow-sized. A dunnock is 14cm long.

What's it like?
A shy female house sparrow, but browner. It also has a thinner, more pointed beak and a darker grey face and front.

What colour is it?
Streaky brown and black on the top, and grey underneath. There's a brownish patch on the side of the head, with grey around it. Its legs are orange-pink. Don't mistake it for a sparrow – have a good look at the shape of its beak.

MORE THAN TWO

Dunnocks have complicated families. There could be two males with one female or two females with a male.

Brown patch on side of head

Thin pointed beak

Grey front

Orange-pink legs

What does it do?

Hides! A dunnock can be hard to see. Look for it moving under bird tables and near bushes, a bit like a mouse. You won't see a flock of dunnocks. Mostly, you will see them on their own.

Streaky brown and black back

What noise does it make?

Its song is gentle, musical and quite fast-moving. It is also very repetitive.

TOP TIP

Listen for the dunnock's song. It often sings from a tree or bush and this makes it easier to see. Sometimes it even sings from rooftops.

Wren

Small and brown but not boring!

How big is it?
Tiny, but it's not our tiniest bird. A wren is about 10cm long and weighs only 10g. Goldcrests and firecrests are our tiniest birds – they weigh a measly 6g.

What's it like?
A small brown blob with a sticky-up tail and a long, sharp bill.

What colour is it?
Brown on top, paler underneath, with thin, dark stripes and pale eyebrows.

Long, sharp beak

Pale eyebrow

Pale front

ROOM FOR ONE MORE?

Small birds find it really hard to stay warm when it's cold. Sometimes lots of wrens pile into the same nestbox to keep each other warm. The record is 63 wrens in one nestbox. You wouldn't want to be at the bottom of that heap!

Sticky-up tail

Darker brown
back

BEST NEST

Female wrens get to choose their nest. The male builds up to five nests. Then the female comes along and picks her favourite.

What does it do?

It often feeds in bushes and other places where it is hard to see. A wren munches its way through loads of insects and spiders. Look for it low down. When a male sings he might do it from a perch a bit higher up. This small bird has a massive voice.

What noise does it make?

Its song is very loud, fast and musical with a rattling trill in it. It also has a loud 'tick' call.

Blue tit

The acrobat.

How big is it?
Smaller than a sparrow.
A blue tit is 12cm long.

What's it like?
Small, fast-moving
and colourful.

What colour is it?
Yellow underneath, with a green
back and blue wings and tail. A blue
tit has a white head with a blue cap,
a black line through the eye and a
small black bib.

What does it do?
A blue tit eats lots of minibeasts as
well as nuts and seeds from bird
feeders. It is light enough to hang on
to thin twigs and sometimes hangs
upside down when it is feeding. In
the winter some go around in flocks
with great tits, long-tailed tits and
other birds. Blue tits often nest in
nestboxes.

What noise does it make?
Its song is two or three high notes
and then a rattle. One of their calls
is a 'churring' noise. Great tits make
a noise like this too.

TOP TIP

Keep an eye out for blue tits
at a seed feeder. They fly to a
feeder, take one seed out and
fly away with it. Then they
come back for more.

Blue tail

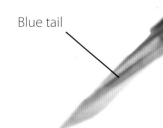

LOOK – I'M A BUTTERFLY!

Sometimes blue tits feed on nectar, just like butterflies. A blue tit sticks its beak into a flower to get at the nectar, or rips the flower off and pecks a hole in it to get a sweet drink.

White head with blue cap

Black line through eye

Green back

Yellow front

Small black bib

Great tit

The teacher bird.

How big is it?
Bigger than a blue tit.
A great tit is about the size
of a sparrow. It's 14cm long.

What's it like?
Bigger than a big blue tit
with a green back, black
and white head and a
black belly stripe.

NOT CATERPILLARS AGAIN

A scientist watched a great tit nest
and counted the number of times the
mum and dad brought food to their
young. In two weeks, they brought
food in 12,685 times! The scientist
must have been very patient.

Green back

Black head with
white cheeks

Yellow front

What colour is it?

Yellow underneath with a black stripe all the way down the front. It has a green back and bluish wings. A great tit's head is black, with white cheeks.

What does it do?

Like a blue tit, it will come to a seed feeder, grab one seed and fly off with it. In the winter, some great tits go around in a gang with other small birds searching for food.

What noise does it make?

It makes lots and lots of different noises! A great tit's song goes 'tea-cher tea-cher tea-cher teach'. That's why it's the teacher bird. One of its many calls is 'pink', which sounds like a chaffinch. They also make a 'churr' like a blue tit.

LOOK AT MY BELLY!

Male great tits have a wider black stripe on their front than the females. The wider the stripe, the more the females fancy the male.

Blue wings

Blue tail

Coal tit

The food-hider.

Black head

White cheeks

How big is it?
The same size as a blue tit.
A coal tit is 12cm long.

What's it like?
Small, plump and fast,
with no bright colours.

Black bib

What colour is it?
Look for the black head with a
white patch on its back, and white
cheeks. A coal tit has two white
stripes on the wing and a dark bib.

TOP TIP

Conifers (evergreen trees) are a good
place to spot coal tits. A coal tit's
small beak is great for pulling out food
in conifers. They can take food from
smaller gaps than blue or great tits.

What does it do?

A coal tit will come to bird feeders for nuts and seeds. It moves around on tree trunks looking for food too. Sometimes it hovers around branches to get food from underneath. Like blue tits and great tits, a coal tit might join a feeding flock in the winter.

What noise does it make?

A coal tit's song goes 'pee-chew pee-chew pee-chew'. Some people think it sounds like a bicycle pump.

DASH AND STASH

If you're a coal tit, blue tits and great tits are the bullies at the bird feeder! So the coal tit nips in, grabs a bit of food, flies off with it, and hides it. It comes back to its secret larder over the next few days to eat in peace!

Long-tailed tit

A ball of feathers on a stick.

How big is it?
Very small, but it has a very long tail. A long-tailed tit is 14cm long, but 9cm of this is its tail.

What's it like?
A flying, feathery lollipop!

What colour is it?
Black and pinkish above and pinky-white underneath. There is some white in its wings and on the edges of its tail. A long-tailed tit's head is white with a thick, black stripe over the eye.

What does it do?
Travels in flocks with other long-tailed tits. It visits bird feeders to scoff peanuts and suet cakes. When a long-tailed tit flies it bounces through the air, going up and down as it moves forward.

What noise does it make?
A long-tailed tit calls a lot. It makes a high 'zee zee zee' and a lower buzzy noise.

White head

Thick black stripe over eye

Pinky-white front

BRILLIANT NEST BUILDERS

It takes over three weeks for these little birds to build a nest. The nest is a hollow ball with a hole for going in and out. They make it from moss and lichen bound together by spider webs. Inside, there are hundreds of feathers to make it nice and cosy.

Black and pinkish back

Long tail

ALL IN THE FAMILY

A long-tailed tit flock is made up of Mum and Dad, their kids, and maybe some aunts and uncles. After a while, the daughters leave and different females move in. If things go wrong for a pair of long-tailed tits, they will split up. Then each one goes and helps out at one of its brother's nests.

Robin

Fiercer than it looks.

How big is it?
About the size of a sparrow.
A robin is 14cm long.

What's it like?
Handsome and often quite tame.

What colour is it?
Brown on top and pale
underneath, with an
orange-red face and
chest. The males and
females look alike but
young robins look
different. They are brown
and mottled instead.

What does it do?
Sings at any time of
the year, unlike most
other birds. It feeds at
bird tables and on the
ground. A robin does a
curtsey when it lands
and will hop rather than
walk. It can look slim,
or much rounder when
it fluffs itself up. Robins
are usually seen on their
own, but sometimes with
one or two others.

TOP TIP

If you want to put up a nestbox for
a robin, it needs to be one with an
open front. They won't squeeze in
through little holes! Learn how
to make a nestbox for robins on
pages 60–61.

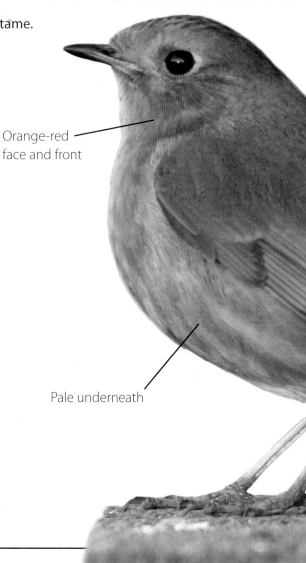

Orange-red
face and front

Pale underneath

WHEN SINGING ISN'T ENOUGH

Most arguments between robins are sorted out quite easily. The robin's song is usually enough to tell other robins to go away. If it doesn't work, they'll show off their red breasts, and make it clear that the 'guest' is not welcome. But sometimes this doesn't work either. The robins fight and it can get really nasty – one of them might be killed.

Brown back

What noise does it make?

A robin's song is musical and fairly slow. They sing to defend the area they want to breed in. When they sing, the males are telling other males to 'clear off!' In the autumn, both male and female robins sing to defend an area for feeding in. The robin's song sounds sadder in the autumn than at other times of the year. Robins also make a 'tick' call.

Blackbird

A wonderful singer and expert worm-catcher.

How big is it?
Bigger than a sparrow, but smaller than a pigeon. A blackbird is 24cm long.

What's it like?
Black and bouncy. Or brown and bouncy!

What colour is it?
The male is a black bird! His beak is orange-yellow. Look for the yellow ring around the eye. The female blackbird is a brown bird! She may have some spots or streaks on her front. Young males have dark beaks and no yellow eye-ring.

TOP SCHOOL BIRD

Blackbirds were the top bird in the Big Schools' Birdwatch in 2010 and 2011. Which other birds do you think made the Schools' top five in 2011? The answers are at the bottom of the page.

IS IT THE SAME ONE?

The blackbirds you see in the winter might not be the same ones you see in the summer. Some come here from northern Europe for the winter and some British blackbirds fly south too. One blackbird might spend the summer in Norfolk and the winter in Devon.

Answer: 2: starling. 3: woodpigeon. 4: black-headed gull. 5: blue tit

What does it do?

Sometimes a blackbird hops across the ground, sometimes it runs. It holds its head on one side to listen for food, before grabbing a worm. It also flicks over leaves with its beak when it is looking for food. A blackbird raises its tail when it lands.

What noise does it make?

The male blackbird is a great singer. Make sure you listen to one. The song is rich, loud, quite slow and musical. If you frighten one, or a cat gets too close, a blackbird makes a loud, rattling alarm call.

Yellow ring around eye

Orange yellow beak

Black body

Song thrush

The 'sing it again' bird.

How big is it?
A bit smaller than a blackbird. A song thrush is 23cm long.

What's it like?
Handsome and spotty.

What colour is it?
Brown on top and pale cream with black spots underneath. The spots are shaped a bit like hearts or like arrow-heads.

What does it do?
Eats worms, other minibeasts and berries. You often see it on the ground looking for food. It finds snails and smashes them to pieces on a rock or path before eating the juicy bits. The song thrush is another loud singer.

What noise does it make?
Its song is loud and rich. It is made up of lots of different lines, and each line is repeated two, three, four or five times before moving on to the next line. One song thrush might have 100 different lines to choose from when he is singing a song.

Pale cream front with black spots

ON THE UP AGAIN?

One of the discoveries of the Big Garden Birdwatch was that song thrush numbers were going down. This may have been because there wasn't as much damp ground on farms as there used to be, so it was harder for them to find food. But it looks like their numbers may be going up again now. That's good news!

Starling

Brilliant mimic and ace formation-flyer.

How big is it?
A bit smaller than a blackbird. A starling is 21cm long.

What's it like?
A shiny, spotty, shorter-tailed blackbird.

What colour is it?
It looks black. However, it also has lots of shiny purple and green in its feathers. Look out for the brown edges on wings and tail too. In the winter starlings have lots of white spots. Young starlings are grey-brown.

What does it do?
Feeds on the ground and squabbles at bird tables! It eats lots of 'leatherjackets'. These are the larvae of crane-flies (daddy-long-legs) and they live in lawns. A starling walks with a waddle. In the winter starlings can be seen in very big flocks. Many thousands roost in the same place.

AIR SHOWS

Forget aeroplanes, starlings are much better at showing off in mid-air. Huge flocks make spectacular shapes in the sky. They fly close to each other, and twist and turn. However they don't bump into each other because they keep a close eye on their neighbours.

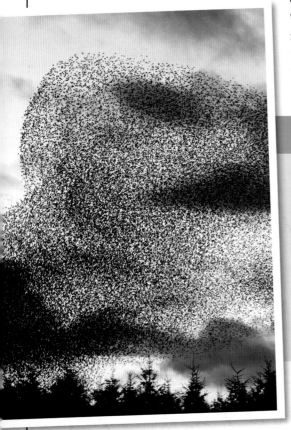

Brown edges on tail

What noise does it make?

All sorts of noises. It is a great mimic and copies many different noises, including other birds and car alarms! A starling's song has whistles, churrs and ticks in it. It makes a stretched out 'chew' noise too.

Black with shiny purple and green in feathers

White spots (in winter)

TOP TIP

During the winter, look out for a starling's white spots. The spots are white tips on their feathers. The tips get worn away over time, so they aren't as spotty in the summer. They grow new feathers with white tips in the autumn.

Pied wagtail

The playground bird.

How big is it?
About as long as a sparrow, but with a long tail.
A pied wagtail is 18cm long.

What's it like?
A fast-running, black and white tail-wagger.

What colour is it?
Pied – which means black and white. There's some grey on it too, especially on females or in the winter.

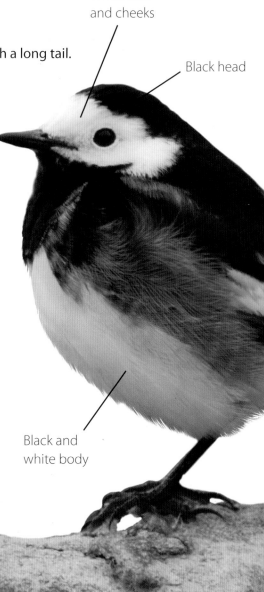

White face and cheeks

Black head

Black and white body

TOP TIP
Watch out for pied wagtails getting together at the end of the afternoon. You might see lots of them in a supermarket car park or on a roof. Then they all head off together to their roost. This could be in a wetland or in trees and bushes in a town. Sometimes hundreds of them roost in the same place.

If a pied wagtail flies over calling, listen to see if a bird on the ground answers. The flying bird is checking to see if anyone else is already on the ground feeding. If they are, the flying wagtail won't bother landing there. The bird that got there first will have eaten all the insects that were easier to catch already.

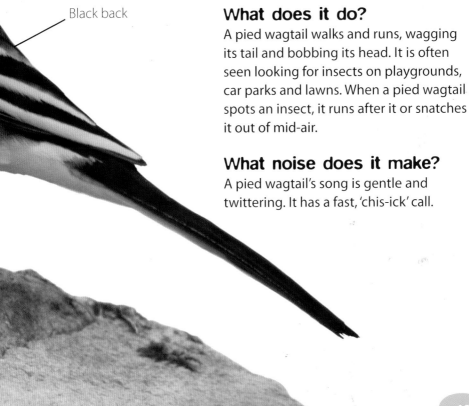

Black back

What does it do?

A pied wagtail walks and runs, wagging its tail and bobbing its head. It is often seen looking for insects on playgrounds, car parks and lawns. When a pied wagtail spots an insect, it runs after it or snatches it out of mid-air.

What noise does it make?

A pied wagtail's song is gentle and twittering. It has a fast, 'chis-ick' call.

Magpie

A black and white crow.

How big is it?
About the size of a pigeon, with a long tail.
A magpie is 45cm long.

What's it like?
A very big, noisy pied wagtail!

What colour is it?
Black and white. But if you look closely
you will also see shiny blue on its
wings and shiny green on its tail.

What does it do?
Goes around on its own or in a small group
with other magpies. The magpie is a bold
character that you see on the ground or
perched in trees and bushes. When it is
on the ground, sometimes it hops and
sometimes it walks. It eats lots of different
things and sometimes takes food from
bird tables. A magpie can be very noisy.

What noise does it make?
A loud chattering.

Black head

White underneath

LONG LIFE MAGPIE

Most magpies live for about
five years. But one is known to
have lived for over 21 years!

NOT ALL CROWS ARE BLACK

Magpies are part of the crow family. So are the carrion crow, rook, jackdaw and jay. Most crows are black, but the magpie and the jay have different colours.

Shiny blue on wings

Shiny green on tail

Carrion crow

A very clever bird.

How big is it?
This is a big bird, bigger than a fat woodpigeon! A carrion crow is 46cm long. It weighs about 500g.

What's it like?
Big and black.

What colour is it?
Black!

CLEVER STUFF

Carrion crows that live near the sea know how to get the juicy bits out of mussels. They grab them, fly up, and drop them onto a rock to smash them open. They have also learned how to get a tasty meal in the Arctic. Fishermen put fishing lines through holes in the ice. A crow comes along, pulls up the line, and takes the bait off the hook! And if a crow finds bread that's a bit too dry, it will put it in some water to make it softer.

What does it do?
A carrion crow finds most of its food on the ground. It will eat all sorts of things. Its main foods are minibeasts and seeds, but it is not a fussy eater. It tucks into animals squashed by traffic. It can dangle on nuts and fat in garden feeders, nick food from other birds, and eat other birds and their eggs too. It even pokes around in rubbish dumps looking for food. On the ground, it hops or walks. Look out for it perched in trees too.

What noise does it make?
A loud 'caw'.

Don't mix up a rook and a carrion crow (left). To help you, have a good look at the feathers on the top of its beak. Unlike carrion crows, rooks don't have feathers on the beak. They have a pale patch on their face instead. Also, a rook is more likely to be in a flock than a carrion crow. Normally you see just one or two carrion crows together.

Black beak

Black body

Rook

The crow that flocks.

How big is it?
About the same size as a carrion crow. A rook is 45cm long.

What's it like?
A carrion crow with a 'bald' beak!

What colour is it?
Black. To tell it from a carrion crow look for a patch of pale skin where its beak joins its face. Some people think a rook looks like an old man!

What does it do?

You often see a rook in a big flock. They feed in farm fields and school playing fields. Look out for their stick nests in the tops of big trees. Lots of rooks nest close together. This is called a rookery. Rooks can make a lot of noise!

Patch of pale skin

Black body

What noise does it make?

A rook goes 'craa'. It sounds similar to a carrion crow. The rook's call is not as harsh as the carrion crow's.

Jackdaw

The cool crow.

How big is it?
A bit smaller than a carrion crow or a rook. A jackdaw is 34cm long.

What's it like?
A small crow with a bright, pale eye.

What colour is it?
Black, with grey on the back of the head and neck. It is easy to see its pale eye.

What does it do?
A jackdaw looks very neat and tidy. It walks with a swagger – like it thinks it's cool! You see it in pairs, in small jackdaw flocks, and in flocks with rooks. It finds most of its food on the ground and eats lots of different things including minibeasts, fruit and seeds. A jackdaw will come into gardens and on to bird tables looking for food too. Watch it flying – it's a great stunt pilot!

What noise does it make?
This one's easy. It says the first part of its name – 'jack, jack'. They also go 'kee-ow'.

CHIMNEY CROW

Jackdaws build their nests in holes, and not just holes in trees. They make themselves at home on rocky cliffs, down rabbit burrows and in big nestboxes. Some of them nest in chimneys. This is not always a good idea – sometimes jackdaws fall down the chimney!

Bright pale eye

Grey on back of head and neck

Black body

STICK AT IT

This cool crow has a simple nest-building method. It finds a stick and drops it down a hole. It keeps dropping sticks down the hole until some of them get stuck. Then it builds its nest on top of them. A pair might spend days dropping sticks before they get anywhere. Some jackdaws have been seen with sticks over 2m long.

Black-headed gull

The gull with the wrong name.

How big is it?

A bit bigger than a pigeon. A black-headed gull is 36cm long.

What's it like?

A noisy bird that looks like it's been in a chocolate pie fight!

What colour is it?

White and grey with black wingtips. In summer it has a chocolate-brown head. For the rest of the year it just has dark smudges. This is why a black-headed gull has the wrong name. It doesn't have a dark head all the time, and when it does, it's brown, not black! The adults' beak and legs are red or reddish. Young birds have more brown in the wings.

TOP TIP

If you want to be a proper bird watcher, call them 'gulls', not 'seagulls'. This makes sense because you can see them a long way from the sea. Black-headed gulls can be seen almost anywhere!

Greyish back
Black wing tips
Reddish legs

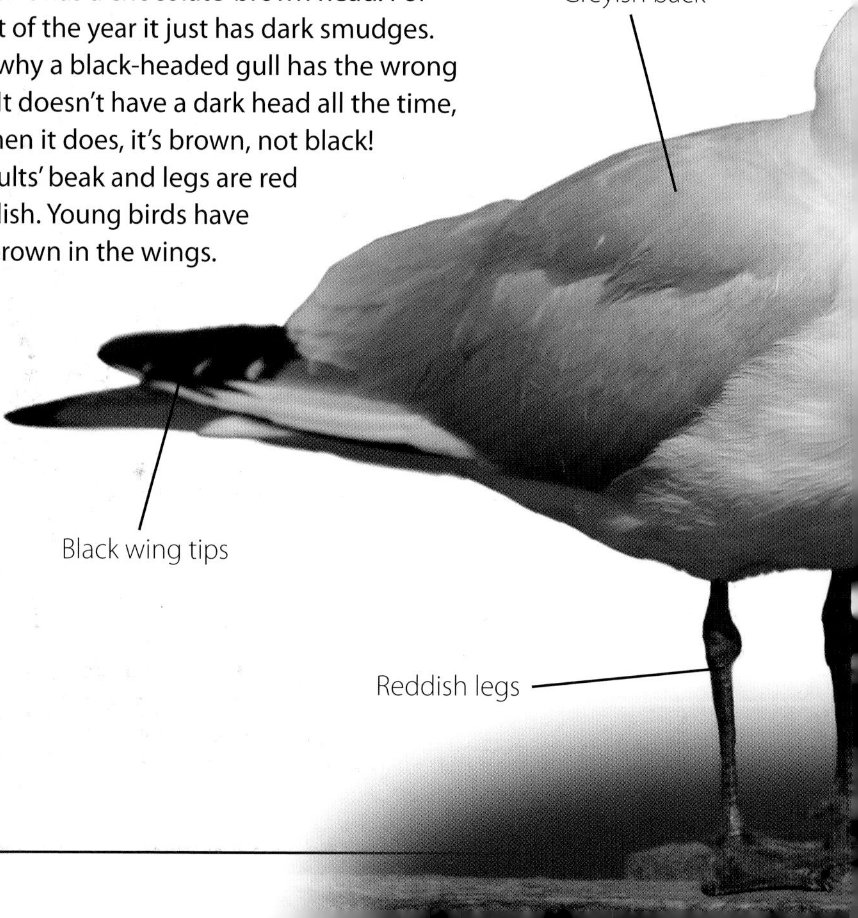

What does it do?

Hangs out on fields. A black-headed gull eats lots of worms. It taps its feet on the ground to trick the worms into coming up. It will also steal food from other birds. You normally see it with other black-headed gulls, sometimes in very large flocks. The flocks make 'V' shapes in the sky when they fly to and from their roosts.

What noise does it make?

A loud, rough 'kreearr'.

FREE-RANGE GULLS

This noisy bird breeds in colonies. That means it makes its nest near to lots of other black-headed gulls. People used to make money by collecting the eggs and selling them for eating. At one place in Norfolk, 1000 eggs could be collected in just one day. That's a lot of omelettes!

Chocolate brown head (in summer)

White front

Common gull

The not-so-common gull!

How big is it?
Bigger than a pigeon and a bit bigger than a black-headed gull. You'll have to look carefully to see the size difference though. A common gull is 41cm long.

What's it like?
A handsome-looking gull with a friendly face!

What colour is it?
Mostly grey and white, with black wingtips with white spots on them. Its beak and legs are yellowy-green. In the winter it has grey smudges on its head. It takes two and a bit years for a common gull to become an adult. Young common gulls have brown on the wings, pinkish legs and a dark stripe on the bill. In the winter, all adults have this dark stripe too.

SHAME ABOUT THE NAME

Because they are not that common! There are lots more black-headed gulls and herring gulls. So why are they called common gulls? It might be because hundreds of years ago, common meant something that had no obvious marks or features.

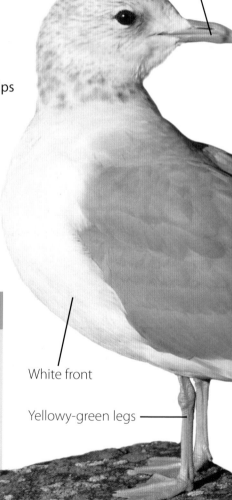

Yellowy-green beak

White front

Yellowy-green legs

A good place to look for gulls is the school field. The nice short grass on the field makes it a good place to go worm hunting. Like black-headed gulls, common gulls tap their feet to trick the worms into coming up. When the worms feel the taps, they hurry to the surface because they think it's raining.

What does it do?

It likes spending time with other gulls. Look at flocks of gulls on a field to see if there are any common gulls among them. You might see them flying over in the morning or at the end of the afternoon. They are travelling between their roost and the place they feed. A common gull may look nice but it doesn't stop it feeding at rubbish dumps! It picks up food in gardens too.

What noise does it make?

It's not always easy describing noises with words – this one is a bit tricky! Common gulls make high-pitched screeches. They cackle as well.

Black wingtips
with white spots

Herring gull

The seaside gull.

How big is it?
Big. Bigger than any of the other birds in this book. A herring gull is 60cm long.

What's it like?
A big, fierce-looking gull.

What colour is it?
An adult herring gull is grey and white, with white spots on black wingtips. It has pink legs, a yellow beak with a red spot on it and staring yellow eyes. In the winter they have grey smudges on the head and neck. It takes just over three years for a herring gull to become an adult. Young ones are mostly brown at first. They get greyer and whiter as they get older.

NOT A FUSSY EATER

Herring gulls eat lots of different things. They'll gobble up fish, minibeasts, fruit, seeds and bits of dead animals. They steal food from other birds, catch mammals to eat and gulp down birds' eggs. To break into crabs and shellfish, they fly up and drop them onto something hard.

Yellow eyes

Yellow beak with a red spot

Pink legs

What does it do?

This is the big, noisy gull you see at the seaside. It's the one that can cause trouble by taking your sandwich out of your hand! You see it away from the coast too. It hangs out in flocks, on land and water. Like other gulls, you see it flying to and from its roost. And like the other gulls, it likes rubbish dumps.

What noise does it make?

The famous seagull noise!

FEED ME!

Chicks peck at the red spot on their parent's beak to say they need feeding. The adult arrives at the nest, the chick pecks at Mum or Dad's beak, and gets a reward... their caring parent coughs up some food for them! Yum.

White spots on black wing tip

Woodpigeon

The wing clatterer.

How big is it?
Bigger than a collared dove or feral pigeon. A woodpigeon is 41cm long.

What's it like?
A fat, bumbling pigeon.

What colour is it?
The easy answer is mostly grey with a white patch on the neck. When it flies, look for a white bar across the wing. However, take a good look at a woodpigeon and you'll see more than grey and white. There's pink on its chest and shiny purple and green on its neck. A young woodpigeon doesn't have the white bit on the neck.

White patch on neck

Shiny purple and green neck

Pink on chest

EGG-STREME!

Most woodpigeons lay their eggs in May and June. Sometimes they lay at other times of the year too. However, if it gets too cold or they think the nest has been found the parents might decide to leave those eggs and have another go.

TOP TIP

Watch out for their roller-coaster display flights. Woodpigeons fly up, give themselves a clap with their wings, then stop flapping and drift down. They might go up and down five times in a row.

Grey back

What does it do?

You might see a woodpigeon alone or in a flock. The flock can be huge, with hundreds of birds in it. It's not very good at sneaking off. Get too close to one in a tree or bush and it flies out with a noisy clatter of wings. A woodpigeon eats seeds, leaves, berries and buds. Look for it on the ground and in trees and bushes. It will come into gardens and on to bird tables. When most birds drink they lift their head so that the water can run down their throat. A woodpigeon sticks its beak in the drink and sucks it up, just like using a straw.

What noise does it make?

It coos. Each sentence has five coos in it.

Collared dove

The cuckoo that isn't.

How big is it?
Pigeon-sized, but smaller than a woodpigeon. A collared is 32cm long.

What's it like?
A pinkish pigeon.

What colour is it?
Mostly pale pinkish-brown. It is called a collared dove because it has a black collar. Its wingtips are black too. Look at the tail on a flying collared dove. It is black near the body, and white at the end. The black collar is harder to see on a young dove.

Black wing tips

NOT A CUCKOO

People get excited when they hear the first cuckoo of spring. It means they can put away their gloves and scarves and get out the sun-cream and sunhats. Cuckoos spend the winter in Africa. They don't normally get back here before the end of March. Sometimes people think they hear a cuckoo before this. Really, they have heard a collared dove going 'coo coo coo', not a cuckoo.

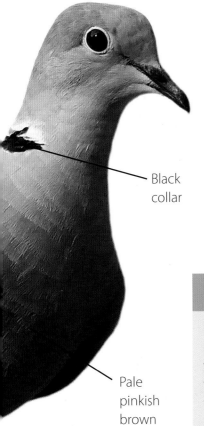

Black collar

Pale pinkish brown

What does it do?

You are likely to see a collared dove on the ground, in a tree, or perched on chimneys, rooftops, aerials or wires. You often see them in pairs, but perhaps also alone or in a flock. It eats loads of seeds and takes food from bird tables. It will also take seed out of seed feeders. If it can't get into the feeder, it might feed on the spilt seed on the ground underneath.

What noise does it make?

It goes coo, like a woodpigeon, but its sentence is slightly different. A collared dove sentence has three coos in it. It also makes a 'kwuuur' noise.

THE NEW COMER

Unlike all the other birds in this book, collared doves have only lived here since the 1950s. They laid their first eggs in this country in 1955. Now you can see them almost anywhere! Since the 1930s, collared doves started to spread west from Turkey, but no-one really knows why.

Feral pigeon

The railway station pigeon.

How big is it?
Pigeon-sized of course! It's about the same size as a collared dove. A feral pigeon is 33cm long.

What's it like?
Scruffy and fearless. This is the town pigeon.

What colour is it?
Feral pigeons come in different colours and different patterns. Some are black and some are white. You will see them with all sorts of patterns, in different shades of grey, black, white and brown.

MORE EGGS?

When there's plenty of food, feral pigeons will lay eggs at almost any time of the year. They normally lay two eggs every time they nest and they can nest five times a year.

TOP TIP

Racing pigeons are the same species. They are taken a long way from home and have to find their way back. You will be able to tell if it is a racing pigeon by the ring on its leg. This ring will be a complete circle with no join (rings on wild birds have a line where the two ends of the metal meet).

What does it do?

It lives in some surprising places. You may see it in railway stations, in city parks and sitting on ledges under bridges. It lives outside towns and cities too. If you see one, there are normally others nearby. A feral pigeon can be very bold. It strolls around picking up crumbs and scraps. It comes very close and might take food out of your hand.

What noise does it make?

A gentle, bubbling coo-ing.

Useful Information

The RSPB speaks out for birds and wildlife, tackling the problems that threaten our environment. Nature is amazing – help us keep it that way. Find out more at **www.rspb.org.uk**

If you enjoy wildlife and want to find out more about it and how you can help it, then RSPB Wildlife Explorers is for you. Become a member and you will receive great magazines, get free entry into our nature reserves and be able to take part in all manner of fun activities. To find out more and to play some great games, visit **www.rspb.org.uk/youth**

Other websites

The Big Schools' Birdwatch
www.rspb.org.uk/schoolswatch

The Big Garden Birdwatch
www.rspb.org.uk/birdwatch

Books

RSPB Children's Guide to Birdwatching
David Chandler and Mike Unwin
A&C Black, 2005

RSPB Pocket Guide to British Birds
Simon Harrap
A&C Black, 2007

RSPB Handbook of British Birds
Peter Holden and Tim Cleeves
Christopher Helm, 2002

Index

Acknowledgements

It's my name on the cover, but I didn't do it on my own. Amy helped with 'Computer art' and 'Acting like a bird'. Thanks Amy. And thanks to Kate for the cuckoo poem and Ruth for her support, and the robin acrostic.

There are lots of RSPB people to thank. Thanks to Mark Boyd and Derek Niemann – for letting me do it, for checking it, and for everything you've done that's made this book better. Thanks also to Richard Bashford, Caroline Offord, Laura Bowman, Val Osborne and Mark Eaton. RSPB Wildlife Explorers wrote the jokes – thank you. And thank you Lynda Whytock for finding them for me.

Finally, I'd better be nice to the publishers. Thank you Elizabeth Jenner. And thanks to Geoff Ward – he made the book look good.

David Chandler